Dedicated to "Splinter" for introducing me to the game of Would You Rather?

Welcome to your very own
"Would You Rather:
Camping and Roadtrip FUN & Trivia" contest!

Get ready for an adventure-packed journey through summer, camping, road trips, holidays, wilderness, bush-craft, and meteorological phenomena.

This book is filled with thrilling "Would you rather" questions and fun facts that will make you the ultimate outdoor expert!

How to Use This Book

- **Gather Your Friends and Family:**

Grab your friends, family, or classmates for some interactive fun.

- **Take Turns Reading Questions:**

Each section has 30 "Would you rather" questions. Take turns reading them and choose your answers.

- **Share Your Answers:**

Explain why you chose your answer. The funniest or smartest answer is the winner and get's their name in the "Winner:" section. Keep track of points!

- **Learn Fun Facts:**

After each question, read the cool trivia to become an outdoor expert.

- **Keep Score:**

Track everyone's points. The person with the most points wins the title of **"Critical Thinker Champ"** and a special certificate.

CONTENT

Super summer

Would you rather

build a giant sandcastle or a giant water slide at the beach?

Winner:

Did you know? The world record for the tallest sandcastle is 57 feet high, which is about as tall as a 5-story building?

• • • • • • • • • •

Would you rather

have a water balloon fight or a super soaker battle?

Winner:

Did you know? A water balloon was once thrown from 109 feet in the air and didn't break until it hit the ground!

Would you rather

spend the day flying kites or riding bikes?

Winner:

Did you know? Kites were originally invented over 2,000 years ago in China, and they were used in battles!

● ● ● ● ● ● ● ● ● ●

Would you rather

go on a treasure hunt in the park or have a picnic with unlimited ice cream?

Winner:

Did you know? The largest picnic ever held included over 22,000 people in Portugal.

Would you rather

swim in a lake with clear blue water or a pool with fun inflatable toys?

Winner:

Did you know? Some of the clearest lakes in the world are so transparent that you can see all the way to the bottom, even if they are very deep!

• • • • • • • • • •

Would you rather

play mini-golf with fun obstacles or go go-kart racing?

Winner:

Did you know? Mini-golf started in Scotland over 100 years ago as a way for women to play golf, which was deemed unsuitable for them on real golf courses.

Would you rather

spend the afternoon bird watching or butterfly catching?

Winner:

Did you know? There are over 10,000 different species of birds worldwide, and some can fly as high as 37,000 feet!

• • • • • • • • • •

Would you rather

have a lemonade stand or a homemade popsicle stand?

Winner:

Did you know? The concept of a lemonade stand started in the 17th century when French vendors sold lemon-flavored drinks on the streets of Paris.

Would you rather

beach volleyball tournament or a frisbee golf championship?

Winner:

Did you know? Beach volleyball started in sunny California in the 1920s and made its Olympic debut in 1996.

• • • • • • • • • •

Would you rather

explore a hidden garden or a new playground?

Winner:

Did you know? The first public playground opened in 1859 in Manchester, England, to give city kids a safe place to play.

Would you rather

fly a kite at the beach or build a boat to float in a stream?

Winner:

Did you know? The largest kite ever flown was as big as a soccer field and required multiple people to control!

• • • • • • • • • •

Would you rather

have a sandcastle building contest or a beach volleyball game?

Winner:

Did you know? Beach volleyball was first played on the beaches of Santa Monica, California, around 1920.

Would you rather

wear sunglasses that let you see underwater or a hat that keeps you cool under any sun?

Winner:

Did you know? Polarized sunglasses were first invented by Edwin H. Land, who used them to reduce glare from water and snow.

• • • • • • • • • •

Would you rather

spend the day at a water park or at a botanical garden?

Winner:

Did you know? The world's largest water park is in Germany and is indoors, covering an area larger than eight football fields!

Would you rather
join a drum circle on the beach or a sing-along around a campfire?

Winner:

Did you know? Drum circles have roots in many cultures and are believed to promote community and wellness through rhythm.

• • • • • • • • • •

Would you rather
discover a secret beach cove or a hidden path in a forest?

Winner:

Did you know? Some of the most beautiful hidden coves in the world are only accessible by hiking or by boat.

Would you rather
eat a picnic lunch on a mountaintop or
by a peaceful lakeside?

Winner:

Did you know? The longest picnic table ever was nearly as long as three football fields. Set up in Poland in 2019, it measured 268.51 meters

• • • • • • • • • •

Would you rather
race jet skis across a lake or race
go-karts on a track?

Winner:

Did you know? Jet skis were first invented in 1973 and can reach speeds over 60 miles per hour.

Would you rather
search for seashells or search for fossils
on the beach?

Winner:

Did you know? Some of the oldest seashells found on beaches can be millions of years old!

● ● ● ● ● ● ● ● ● ●

Would you rather
have a magic carpet that flies or
a bike that can ride on water?

Winner:

Did you know? The idea of a magic carpet has been popular in tales and folklore, notably in stories like "Aladdin" from "One Thousand and One Nights."

Would you rather
go horseback riding on the beach at sunrise or paddleboarding at sunset?

Winner:

Did you know? Horses can sleep standing up thanks to a special mechanism in their legs, allowing them to quickly escape predators even while napping!

• • • • • • • • • •

Would you rather
eat only ice cream for a day or only fruit for a day while at the beach?

Winner:

Did you know? The world's largest bowl of ice cream weighed over 12 tons and was made in Edmonton, Canada.

Would you rather
swim with dolphins in the ocean or go bird watching at the shore?

Winner:

Did you know? Dolphins have names for each other? They use unique whistles to identify and call each other, just like humans use names!

• • • • • • • • • •

Would you rather
climb a lighthouse to see the view or explore a submarine submerged near the shore?

Winner:

Did you know? The first successful submarine was built in 1620 by Cornelius Drebbel, commissioned by King James I of England.

Would you rather
play a game of beach frisbee or beach soccer?

Winner:

Did you know? Beach soccer balls are lighter and bigger than regular ones, making it easier to play on sandy and windy beaches.

• • • • • • • • • •

Would you rather
find a message in a bottle on the beach or discover a buried treasure chest?

Winner:

Did you know? The oldest message in a bottle was found after 108 years at sea, launched in 1906 for a study on ocean currents.

Would you rather
have a super soaker fight or a mud pie making contest?

Winner

Did you know? The Super Soaker was invented by a NASA engineer, who was originally working on a new type of heat pump.

• • • • • • • • • •

Would you rather
create a giant piece of beach art from stones and shells or build a detailed sand sculpture?

Winner:

Did you know? The world's tallest sandcastle, built in Germany in 2019, stood over 57 feet high and used 11,000 tons of sand.

Would you rather
participate in a beach cleanup or plant trees in a local park?

Winner:

Did you know? In Mumbai, India, volunteers removed over 5.3 million kilograms (as heavy as 890 elepants) of trash from a beach helping bab turtles reach the sea for the first time in decade

• • • • • • • • • •

Would you rather
have a day of unlimited paddleboat rides or unlimited rollercoaster rides at a beachside amusement park?

Winner:

Did you know? Paddleboats can have built-in water guns for exciting water battles while you pedal around the lake!

CRAZY

camping

Would you rather
sleep in a tent or
under the stars?

Winner:

Did you know? that the largest tent ever recorded was almost as big as a football field?

● ● ● ● ● ● ● ● ● ●

Would you rather
roast marshmallows or cook hot dogs over the campfire?

Winner:

Did you know? Marshmallows were originally made from the root of the marshmallow plant, which was believed to have healing properties.

Would you rather
go on a night hike with flashlights or
stay by the campfire telling stories?

Winner:

Did you know? Fireflies, often seen during night hikes, aren't flies at all; they are beetles and there are over 2,000 species of them!

• • • • • • • • • •

Would you rather
explore a nearby cave or fish in a nearby stream?

Winner:

Did you know? The deepest cave in the world is in the country of Georgia and is 7,208 feet deep, which is more than 1.3 miles!

Would you rather
participate in a campsite scavenger hunt or a bird-watching competition?

Winner:

Did you know? The peregrine falcon, which can be spotted during bird watching, is the fastest bird and can dive at speeds over 240 miles per hour!

● ● ● ● ● ● ● ● ● ●

Would you rather
build a campfire or set up a solar-powered campsite?

Winner:

Did you know? The first recorded campfire was over 1 million years ago, and people have been gathering around them for warmth and community ever since.

Would you rather
sleep in a sleeping bag on the ground or in a hammock?

Winner:

Did you know? Hammocks were developed by native inhabitants of Central and South America for sleeping. They were later used by sailors for comfort and to maximize space.

• • • • • • • • • •

Would you rather
have a campsite pizza party with a portable oven or a barbecue night?

Winner:

Did you know? The world's largest barbecue cooked thousands of pounds of meat and fed over 45,000 people!

Would you rather
go searching for fireflies at dusk or stargazing at midnight?

Winner:

Did you know? Stargazing can help you see stars, planets, and even the Milky Way if the sky is clear and you're far from city lights.

• • • • • • • • • •

Would you rather
wake up early for a sunrise hike or stay up late for a nocturnal wildlife tour?

Winner:

Did you know? Nocturnal animals, like owls and foxes, have special adaptations like enhanced hearing and night vision to help them see in the dark.

Would you rather
find a geocache hidden in the forest or discover a new species of plant?

Winner:

Did you know? Geocaching is a real-world, outdoor treasure hunting game using GPS-enabled devices, and there are millions of geocaches hidden around the world!

● ● ● ● ● ● ● ● ● ●

Would you rather
make a whistle from a chestnut branch or a necklace from forest finds?

Answer:

Did you know? The loudest whistle ever recorded reached 125.8 decibels, as loud as a rock concert, set by a man in the UK in 2015.

Would you rather
help set up a rope bridge across a creek or a zip line between trees?

Winners:

Did you know? The longest zip line in the world is over 1.76 miles long and reaches speeds of up to 93 miles per hour!

• • • • • • • • • •

Would you rather
take photos of wildlife or draw the landscape around your campsite?

Answer:

Did you know? Wildlife photographers use camera traps to automatically snap photos of shy or rare animals when they pass by, without needing to be there!

Would you rather
rather sleep next to a waterfall or on a mountain top?

Winner:

Did you know? The sound of waterfalls has been shown to naturally soothe the mind and can help promote better sleep.

• • • • • • • • • •

Would you rather
have a campfire quiz night or a silent reading time by lantern light?

Winner:

Did you know? Lanterns were first used in ancient China around 250 BC and were made from silk, paper, and bamboo.

Would you rather
paddle a canoe down a calm river or raft through mild rapids?

Winner:

Did you know? The world's oldest canoe, found in the Netherlands, is about 10,000 years old and was made from a single hollowed-out log during the Stone Age!

• • • • • • • • • •

Would you rather
use a map and compass for a day hike or a GPS device?

Winner:

Did you know? The compass was invented by the Chinese during the Han Dynasty between the 2nd century BC and 1st century AD.

Would you rather
spot a deer family near your campsite or find a rare bird's nest?

Winner:

Did you know? Deer are very cautious animals and can detect movement from up to 100 meters away.

• • • • • • • • • •

Would you rather
participate in a wilderness survival workshop or an environmental conservation project?

Winner:

Did you know? Conservation efforts have successfully brought numerous species back from the brink of extinction, like the American Bald Eagle.

Would you rather
cook a meal over an open fire or prepare a meal using only solar cooking tools?

Winner:

Did you know? Solar cookers use the sun's energy to heat food, which can reach temperatures hot enough to cook just like a conventional oven.

• • • • • • • • • •

Would you rather
create an obstacle course in the woods or set up a series of nature trivia stations along a trail?

Winner:

Did you know? Obstacle courses have been used in military training since ancient times to prepare soldiers for physical challenges.

Would you rather
lead a group hike with a flag or follow with a walkie-talkie to communicate?

Winner:

Did you know? Walkie-talkies were first used in military communications during World War II and have become popular in many outdoor activities for keeping groups connected.

• • • • • • • • • •

Would you rather
build a stone cairn at a trailhead or a wooden signpost?

Winner:

Did you know? Stone cairns, stacks of rocks on trails, have been used as markers for thousands of years and are a tradition older than the pyramids!

Would you rather
have an outdoor skills challenge day or a creative arts and crafts day using natural materials?

Winner:

Did you know? In places like Uganda, craftspeople make eco-friendly paper from dried banana fibers, using them for drawing, writing, and crafts!

● ● ● ● ● ● ● ● ● ●

Would you rather
watch a sunset from a hilltop or a sunrise over a lake?

Winner:

Did you know? Sunsets often appear more colorful than sunrises due to the angle of the sun and increased particles in the air by evening.

Would you rather
track animal footprints or identify different types of trees?

Winner:

Did you know? Tracking has been essential for human survival for thousands of years, helping to find food and avoid predators.

• • • • • • • • • •

Would you rather
build a fort out of branches and leaves or dig a small pond?

Winner:

Did you know? Ponds have a day-night rhythm where plants produce oxygen during the day and consume it at night, much like how we breathe!

Would you rather
participate in a campsite relay race or a group yoga session in nature?

Winner:

Did you know? Yoga originated over 5,000 years ago and practicing in nature can enhance feelings of tranquility and connection to the earth.

● ● ● ● ● ● ● ● ● ●

Would you rather
sing campfire songs with a guitar or listen to a park ranger tell stories about the park

Winner:

Did you know? Park rangers employ advanced gadgets similar to superhero gear, like night vision goggles and specialized radios, to ensure the welfare of animals in remote areas.

ROADTRIP READY

Would you rather
take a road trip across the desert or through a lush green forest?

Winner:

Did you know? The largest desert in the world, the Sahara, is almost as big as the entire United States!

● ● ● ● ● ● ● ● ● ●

Would you rather
travel in a vintage camper van or a modern RV?

Winner:

Did you know? The first motorized campers were built in 1910, and they have been a favorite for road trip enthusiasts ever since.

Would you rather
stop at a famous national park or a hidden gem local park?

Winner:

Did you know? Yellowstone was the first national park in the world, established in 1872.

• • • • • • • • • •

Would you rather
have a picnic at a roadside rest area or a local diner?

Winner:

Did you know? The first drive-in restaurant opened in 1921 in Dallas, Texas, revolutionizing how Americans eat during road trips.

Would you rather
listen to an audiobook or your favorite music playlist while driving?

Winner:

Did you know? The first audiobook was created in 1932 for people who were visually impaired.

• • • • • • • • • •

Would you rather
go on a road trip to see a meteor shower or a solar eclipse?

Winner:

Did you know? A solar eclipse can last for over 7 minutes in one location, but each location on Earth sees a solar eclipse approximately every 375 years.

Would you rather
drive along the coast with ocean views or through the mountains with scenic peaks?

Winner:

Did you know? The Pacific Coast Highway in California offers stunning views of the ocean and is considered one of the most beautiful drives in the world.

• • • • • • • • • •

Would you rather
explore a big city or discover small towns along your route?

Winner:

Did you know? Some of the smallest towns in America have populations of fewer than 10 people!

Would you rather
visit a famous museum or go to an amusement park during your road trip?

Winner:

Did you know? The Smithsonian in Washington D.C. is the largest museum complex in the world, with over 19 museums and galleries.

• • • • • • • • • •

Would you rather
camp in a national park or stay in a quirky roadside motel?

Winner:

Did you know? The USA's national parks cover over 84 million acres, which is larger than the country of Germany.

Would you rather
have a road trip theme song that is a pop hit or
a classic rock anthem?

Winner

Did you know? Queen's "Bohemian Rhapsody" is one of the most popular road trip songs ever, thanks to its dramatic shifts

• • • • • • • • • •

Would you rather
drive through a forest with giant trees or across a vast desert?

Winner:

Did you know? Some giant sequoia trees in California are over 3,000 years old and taller than a 26-story building!

Would you rather
stop at a famous ice cream shop in every town or try a new snack from each place?

Winner:

Did you know? Ice cream was first made in China around 200 BCE with snow, fruit, and honey.

● ● ● ● ● ● ● ● ● ●

Would you rather
visit a volcano or a deep-sea aquarium on your road trip?

Winner:

Did you know? The deepest part of the ocean is the Mariana Trench, which is deeper than Mount Everest is tall!

Would you rather
have a map that shows hidden treasures or one that leads to secret magical spots?

Winner:

Did you know? The concept of a treasure map was popularized by the novel "Treasure Island" by Robert Louis Stevenson.

• • • • • • • • • •

Would you rather
camp under the stars every night or stay in a different themed hotel room each night?

Winner:

Did you know? There are hotels that offer rooms under the sea, complete with views of fish and other ocean life swimming by!

Would you rather
travel by a funky painted bus or a speedy sports car?

Winner:

Did you know? The Volkswagen bus, often painted with colorful designs, became a symbol of the hippie movement in the 1960s.

• • • • • • • • • •

Would you rather
find a dinosaur fossil or a rare gemstone during a roadside stop?

Winner:

Did you know? There are over 3,800 known ghost towns in the United States, most abandoned after booms in mining and gold rushes.

Would you rather
have an unlimited supply of books or games for the road trip?

Answer:

Did you know? The world's largest library, the Library of Congress, has over 170 million items!

• • • • • • • • • •

Would you rather
travel through time at each stop or stay in the present and learn the history?

Answer:

Did you know? Traveling at light speed could slow time around you according to the theory of relativity, so you might return from a space trip to meet your future grandkids!

Would you rather
sing along to rock classics or the latest pop hits on the radio?

Winner:

Did you know? The song "Hey Jude" by The Beatles was one of the longest singles ever to top the British charts, running over seven minutes.

• • • • • • • • • •

Would you rather
explore a cave filled with crystals or a forest with trees that glow in the dark?

Winner:

Did you know?There are bioluminescent organisms, like certain fungi and bacteria, that can make trees and other objects appear to glow in the dark.

Would you rather
meet a famous inventor or a famous explorer at a roadside museum?

Winner:

Did you know? Leonardo da Vinci, a famous inventor, sketched ideas for inventions like helicopters and tanks centuries before they were actually made.

● ● ● ● ● ● ● ● ● ●

Would you rather
have a picnic on a mountaintop or next to a giant waterfall?

Winner:

Did you know? Angel Falls in Venezuela is the world's highest uninterrupted waterfall, with a height of 979 meters (3,212 ft).

Would you rather
discover a new animal species or find an ancient artifact?

Winner:

Did you know? Over 15,000 new species are discovered each year, ranging from tiny insects to large mammals.

• • • • • • • • • •

Would you rather
ride a mountain gondola or a river ferry as part of your road trip?

Winner:

Did you know? The highest cable car in the world reaches 5,029 meters above sea level in the mountains of China.

Would you rather
participate in a local festival or a sporting event while visiting a town?

Winner:

Did you know? The largest food festival in the world is La Tomatina in Spain, where participants throw over 150,000 tomatoes at each other.

● ● ● ● ● ● ● ● ● ●

Would you rather
create an epic travel vlog or a digital photo album of your road trip adventures?

Winner:

Did you know? The first digital camera was developed in 1975 and took 23 seconds to capture its first image.

Would you rather
try exotic foods at each stop or stick to your favorite comfort foods?

Winner:

Did you know? The durian, known as the "king of fruits," is famous in Southeast Asia for its large size, strong odor, and unique taste.

• • • • • • • • • •

Would you rather
attend a car show featuring classic cars or futuristic vehicles?

Winner:

Did you know? The first car, the Benz Patent Motorwagen, was built in 1885 and had a top speed of 10 miles per hour.

Holiday
HURRY

Would you rather
spend Christmas in a snowy cabin or a beach house?

Winner:

Did you know? Snow acts as an insulator; that's why some animals hibernate in snow to stay warm during winter.

● ● ● ● ● ● ● ● ● ●

Would you rather
have a Halloween party in a haunted castle or in a spooky forest?

Winner:

Did you know? The largest haunted house in the world is located in Ohio and covers over 52 acres.

Would you rather
celebrate New Year's Eve in Times Square or at home with a big party?

Winner:

Did you know? The Times Square New Year's Eve ball weighs about 11,875 pounds and is covered in over 2,688 crystals.

● ● ● ● ● ● ● ● ● ●

Would you rather
go egg hunting on Easter in a large amusement park or in your backyard with secret tunnels?

Winner:

Did you know? The term "Easter" gets its name from Eastre, the Anglo-Saxon goddess who symbolizes the hare and the egg.

Would you rather
celebrate New Year's Eve in Times Square or at home with a big party?

Winner:

Did you know? The Times Square New Year's Eve ball weighs about 11,875 pounds and is covered in over 2,688 crystals.

• • • • • • • • • •

Would you rather
go egg hunting on Easter in a large amusement park or in your backyard with secret tunnels?

Winner:

Did you know? the world's largest Easter egg was over 34 feet high and weighed nearly 8,000 pounds, and it was made in Italy in 2011.

Would you rather
spend your summer vacation in Disneyland or on a safari in Africa?

Winner:

Did you know? Disneyland has a secret apartment above the fire station on Main Street where Walt Disney used to stay.

• • • • • • • • • •

Would you rather
go on a holiday to the North Pole to meet Santa Claus or to the Bahamas?

Winner:

Did you know? The North Pole is warmer in winter than the South Pole because it's surrounded by sea, which holds heat better than ice.

Would you rather
travel back in time for the first Thanksgiving or forward in time to a future space holiday celebration?

Winner:

Did you know? The first Thanksgiving was celebrated in 1621 and lasted three days.

• • • • • • • • • •

Would you rather
have a water balloon fight on the Fourth of July or a snowball fight on Christmas?

Winner:

Did you know? The highest recorded temperature on the Fourth of July in the USA was 134 degrees Fahrenheit in Death Valley, California.

Would you rather
spend a week at a holiday camp with magic lessons or ninja training?

Winner:

Did you know? Ninjas used special shoes called "jika-tabi" that helped them move silently.

• • • • • • • • • •

Would you rather
explore the pyramids of Egypt during your spring break or the rainforests of the Amazon?

Winner:

Did you know? The Great Pyramid of Giza was the tallest man-made structure in the world for over 3,800 years.

Would you rather
attend a colorful Diwali festival in India or a vibrant Carnival in Brazil?

Winner:

Did you know? Diwali is known as the Festival of Lights and is celebrated by millions of people across the world.

• • • • • • • • • •

Would you rather
have a traditional Japanese tea ceremony on New Year's Day or a barbecue on Independence Day?

Winner:

Did you know? Did you know that during a Japanese tea ceremony, some sweets are served that are shaped like flowers or animals, and they're almost too cute to eat?

Would you rather
spend Thanksgiving Day playing football or on a treasure hunt in your neighborhood?

Winner:

Did you know? The concept of Thanksgiving football games started with Yale versus Princeton in 1876.

• • • • • • • • • •

Would you rather
go to a chocolate factory during Easter holidays or to a toy factory before Christmas?

Winner:

Did you know? The world's largest chocolate factory is in Belgium, which produces over 270,000 tons of chocolate every year.

Would you rather
visit Santa's workshop in the North Pole or the Easter Bunny's garden?

Winner:

Did you know? Male reindeers shed their antlers in winter, so all of Santa's reindeer, including Rudolph, are likely female or young.

• • • • • • • • • •

Would you rather
have a midnight feast under the Northern Lights or a picnic under the midday sun in a desert?

Winner:

Did you know? The Northern Lights are caused by particles from the sun colliding with the Earth's atmosphere.

Would you rather
join a Viking festival in Scandinavia or a medieval tournament in England?

Winner:

Did you know? Vikings were known to host large feasts that could last for days.

• • • • • • • • • •

Would you rather
swim with dolphins during a summer holiday or go dog sledding during winter vacation?

Winner:

Did you know? Dog sled teams can run up to 100 miles a day in races, and the lead dogs are so smart they can find trails under thick snow?

Would you rather
watch fireworks in Japan during Tanabata or in the USA on the Fourth of July?

Winner:

Did you know? During Tanabata, a Japanese star festival, people write their wishes on colorful strips of paper and hang them on bamboo trees, hoping the stars will make them come true.

• • • • • • • • • •

Would you rather
be part of a parade on Mardi Gras in New Orleans or at the Carnival in Venice?

Winner:

Did you know? Mardi Gras is also known as "Pancake Day" in many places, and people have pancake eating contests and races where they run while flipping pancakes in a pan.

Would you rather
spend a day at the historic sites of Rome during Christmas or at the sunny beaches of Sydney?

Winner:

Did you know? Rome is known as the "Eternal City," a term coined by ancient Romans who believed that no matter what happened to the world, Rome would go on forever.

● ● ● ● ● ● ● ● ● ●

Would you rather
have a surfing lesson in Hawaii or a skiing lesson in the Swiss Alps?

Winner:

Did you know? Hawaii is the only U.S. state that grows coffee commercially, and it's famous for its unique and flavorful Kona coffee.

Would you rather
join a holiday expedition to find the lost city of Atlantis or search for pirate treasure in the Caribbean?

Winner:

Did you know? Legend says Atlantis was an advanced island with robots, flying machines, and powerful crystals, and could control the weather.

● ● ● ● ● ● ● ● ● ●

Would you rather
ride a camel around the pyramids in Egypt or a gondola in Venice during your summer holiday?

Winner:

Did you know? Venice is built on more than 100 small islands and has over 400 bridges connecting them.

Would you rather
visit a castle in Scotland during a foggy autumn or a lighthouse in Maine during a stormy spring?

Winner:

Did you know? The Edinburgh Castle in Scotland is built on an extinct volcano and is one of the oldest fortified places in Europe.

● ● ● ● ● ● ● ● ● ●

Would you rather
attend the opening ceremony of the Olympics in Tokyo or the FIFA World Cup final in Brazil?

Winner:

Did you know? The Olympic Games originated over 3,000 years ago in the plains of Olympia, Greece.

Would you rather
spend a white Christmas in Moscow or a sunny Christmas in Australia?

Winner:

Did you know? In Australia, Christmas comes in the middle of summer, so many people celebrate with a barbecue on the beach.

● ● ● ● ● ● ● ● ● ●

Would you rather
help build a giant sandcastle at a beach festival or a giant snowman at a winter festival?

Answer:

Did you know? The world's largest snowman was built in Maine and stood 122 feet tall, which is as high as a 12-story building?

Wilderness
WONDERS

Would you rather
rather explore a deep jungle with a machete or a desert with a camel?

Winner:

Did you know? Jungles can have up to 80 inches of rain a year!

• • • • • • • • • •

Would you rather
climb the tallest mountain or dive in the deepest part of the ocean?

Answer:

Did you know? Mount Everest is over 29,000 feet tall, taller than the cruising altitude of most passenger planes!

Would you rather
spend the night in a treehouse in a rainforest or in an igloo in the Arctic?

Winner:

Did you know? Igloos can be warmer inside than outside during winter, sometimes reaching 60°F inside while it's freezing outside, due to body heat and insulating power of snow?

• • • • • • • • • •

Would you rather
track a lion in Africa or a bear in North America?

Winner:

Did you know? A lion's roar can be heard from up to 5 miles away, making it one of the loudest sounds produced by any animal in the wild.

Would you rather
have a pet falcon or a pet wolf while adventuring in the wild?

Winner:

Did you know? Falcons are among the fastest birds, reaching speeds of over 200 mph during a dive!

● ● ● ● ● ● ● ● ● ●

Would you rather
navigate a river by kayak or by canoe?

Winner:

Did you know? Kayaks were originally developed by the Inuit in the Arctic region for hunting!

Would you rather
walk through a forest with 100-year-old trees or a new forest growing after a fire?

Winner:

Did you know? Forest fires sometimes help by clearing old trees and enabling new growth!

• • • • • • • • • •

Would you rather
go on a safari to see elephants or go whale watching?

Winner:

Did you know? Elephants are the largest land animals, while blue whales are the largest animals in the world!

Would you rather
find a hidden waterfall or
a secret cave?

Winner:

Did you know? The largest cave chamber in the world is in Malaysia, large enough to fit 40 Boeing 747s!

• • • • • • • • • •

Would you rather
hike a trail that leads to ancient ruins or to a hidden lake?

Winner:

Did you know? Some ancient ruins are over thousands of years old and were only rediscovered recently!

Would you rather
try rock climbing or zip-lining through a forest?

Winner:

Did you know? Zip-lining was originally created to help scientists quickly move between areas in dense rainforests!

• • • • • • • • • •

Would you rather
be able to talk to animals or have plants grow instantly at your command while exploring?

Winner:

Did you know? Some plants can communicate with each other through their root systems!

Would you rather
camp on a beach or on
the side of a cliff?

Winner:

Did you know? Cliff camping involves sleeping in a tent that hangs off the side of a cliff!

• • • • • • • • • •

Would you rather
try ice fishing in the Arctic or
desert sandboarding?

Winner:

Did you know? Sandboarding is like snowboarding but on sand dunes!

Would you rather
have a campfire in the woods or on a snowy mountain?

Winner:

Did you know? Campfires can reach scorching temperatures up to 2,000 degrees Fahrenheit–that's hot enough to melt some types of metal!

• • • • • • • • • •

Would you rather
paddleboard on a calm lake or surf on ocean waves?

Winner:

Did you know? Paddleboarding can boost your balance skills because it requires you to stand up straight on a board while floating on water, just like a superhero on a mission

Would you rather
go bird watching in the Amazon or animal spotting in the savannah?

Winner:

Did you know? The Amazon rainforest is one of the most biodiverse places on Earth!

• • • • • • • • • •

Would you rather
swim in a crystal-clear tropical sea or a fresh mountain stream?

Answer:

Did you know? Mountain streams are often so clear because they are fed by underground springs!

Would you rather
ride a horse across open plains or an elephant through a jungle?

Winner:

Did you know? Elephants can communicate with each other using sounds that humans can't hear!

• • • • • • • • • •

Would you rather
go treasure hunting in an old forest or deep-sea diving for sunken ships?

Winner:

Did you know? There are more than 3 million shipwrecks on the ocean floor!

Would you rather
face a simulated earthquake or a simulated tornado on
an adventure trip?

Winner:

Did you know? Earthquakes can release more energy than thousands of atomic bombs!

• • • • • • • • • •

Would you rather
be an expert at surviving in the desert or the rainforest?

Winner:

Did you know? Rainforests cover less than 3% of Earth's surface but hold more than 50% of its wildlife

Would you rather
encounter a school of dolphins or a group of friendly monkeys during your adventure?

Winner:

Did you know? Dolphins love to play games like "catch" with seaweed and even blow bubble rings for fun!

● ● ● ● ● ● ● ● ● ●

Would you rather
try living in a snowy cabin in the woods for a week or in a jungle treehouse?

Winner:

Did you know? Treehouses can be equipped with pulley systems to bring up snacks and supplies, turning them into awesome treetop fortresses!

Would you rather
participate in a mountain bike race or a canoeing marathon?

Winner:

Did you know? Mountain biking originated in California in the 1970s as an off-road sport!

● ● ● ● ● ● ● ● ● ●

Would you rather
wear a suit of armor or a stealthy ninja outfit on a quest through the forest?

Winner:

Did you know? Ninjas were skilled in the Japanese art of stealth called "ninjutsu" during feudal times!

Would you rather
be able to breathe underwater or have the ability to fly when exploring nature?

Winner:

Did you know? The pressure at the bottom of the Mariana Trench is so intense that it's like having about 50 jumbo jets pressing down on every square inch of your body.

• • • • • • • • • •

Would you rather
go searching for ancient artifacts in Egypt or fossils in the Badlands?

Winner:

Did you know? The largest dinosaur fossils have been found in the Badlands of North America!

Would you rather
experience a day as a polar bear in the Arctic or as a kangaroo in the Australian Outback?

Winner:

Did you know? Kangaroos can leap over 3 times their height in a single bound!

● ● ● ● ● ● ● ● ● ●

Would you rather
explore a mysterious island by yourself or with a team of other adventurers?

Winner:

Did you know? Explorers like Jane Goodall ventured into the jungles of Africa to study chimpanzees, unlocking secrets about their behavior and communication!

Bushcraft Basics

Would you rather
build a shelter from branches and leaves or fashion a fishing spear from natural materials?

WinnerL

Did you know? Some birds use spider silk to weave their nests for added strength and flexibility.

• • • • • • • • • •

Would you rather
forage for wild berries or learn to start a fire without matches?

Winner:

Did you know? The ancient technique of fire starting using a bow drill dates back thousands of years.

Would you rather
navigate using the stars or make a compass out of natural materials?

Winner:

Did you know? Vikings used a special stone called a sunstone to navigate on cloudy days by locating the position of the sun.

• • • • • • • • • •

Would you rather
purify water using a solar still or construct a snare trap for small game?

Winner:

Did you know? Cattail plants can be used to filter water due to their dense, fibrous roots.

Would you rather
create a map of your surroundings or learn to identify edible plants in the wild?

Winner:

Did you know? The art of mapmaking, or cartography, has been practiced for thousands of years, with some of the earliest maps dating back to ancient Babylon.

• • • • • • • • • •

Would you rather
make a bow and arrow or construct a primitive fishing net?

Winner:

Did you know? In the Arctic, Inuit kids slide down snowy hills on sleds made from frozen fish to have a slippery and thrilling ride!

Would you rather
learn to make natural cordage from plant fibers
or a whistle from wood?

Winner:

Did you know? The inner bark of certain trees, like the basswood, can be stripped and twisted to make strong and flexible cordage.

● ● ● ● ● ● ● ● ● ●

Would you rather
build a primitive oven for baking or
a container to boil water?

Winner:

Did you know? Native American tribes often used woven baskets lined with clay to boil water and cook food.

Would you rather
create a natural insect repellent or a torch for nighttime exploration?

Winner:

Did you know? Citronella, a plant known for its insect-repelling properties, has been used for centuries by various cultures to keep bugs at bay.

• • • • • • • • • •

Would you rather
construct a basic shelter using a tarp or a makeshift utensil for cooking?

Winner:

Did you know? The Bedouin people of the desert often use simple tents called "black tents" made from goat hair for their nomadic lifestyle.

Would you rather
learn to tie various knots for survival or make a container from birch bark?

Winner:

Did you know? The art of knot tying, or "knotcraft," has a long history and was essential for sailors, climbers, and hunters alike.

• • • • • • • • • •

Would you rather
make a natural toothbrush from twigs or a sling for hunting small animals?

Winner:

Did you know? The ancient Egyptians are believed to have used twigs from the Salvadora persica tree as early forms of toothbrushes.

Would you rather
learn to identify different types of clouds or make a simple raft for crossing a river?

Winner:

Did you know? Cloud formations can provide valuable information about impending weather changes, aiding in survival situations.

• • • • • • • • • •

Would you rather
learn to make a container to collect rainwater or learn to make a whistle from a hollow reed?

Winner:

Did you know? Bamboo, with its hollow segments, is often used to make various tools and instruments, including whistles.

Would you rather
learn to make natural dyes from plants or
construct a makeshift fishing rod?

Winner:

Did you know? Ancient civilizations, like the Egyptians, used crushed insects called cochineal to make vibrant red dyes.

• • • • • • • • • •

Would you rather
build a natural refrigerator using cool underground storage or a simple trap for catching fish?

Winner:

Did you know? Some ancient civilizations, like the Persians, used underground storage chambers called "yakhchāl" to store ice and food.

Would you rather
learn to make natural soap from plant oils or a solar cooker for outdoor cooking?

Winner:

Did you know? Solar cookers use reflective surfaces to concentrate sunlight, converting it into heat energy for cooking food.

• • • • • • • • • •

Would you rather
create a natural toothpaste from baking soda and mint leaves or learn to make a fishing spear from wood?

Winner:

Did you know? Baking soda, a common household item, has been used for centuries for its cleansing properties and can be combined with mint for fresh breath.

Would you rather
learn to make a simple fishing hook from bone or construct a trap to catch insects for protein?

Winner:

Did you know? Some indigenous cultures use dried fish bones, shaped into hooks, for catching fish in rivers and streams.

• • • • • • • • • •

Would you rather
learn to make a whistle from a blade of grass or fashion a makeshift compass using a magnetized needle?

Winner:

Did you know? Grass whistles are made by holding a blade of grass tightly between your thumbs and blowing air through it, creating a high-pitched sound.

Would you rather
learn to make a torch using animal fat or use the animal fat to make soap?

Winner:

Did you know? Animal fat, particularly from animals like deer or bears, has been used historically as a fuel source for lamps and torches.

● ● ● ● ● ● ● ● ● ●

Would you rather
create a natural mosquito repellent from essential oils or make a natural suncreen using natural oils?

Winner:

Did you know? Some plants, like aloe vera and coconut oil, contain natural SPF properties and have been used for centuries to protect skin from the sun.

Would you rather
construct a simple water filtration system using sand and gravel or one with moss and charcoal?

Winner:

Did you know? Moss has natural antibacterial properties and has been used in wound dressings by ancient cultures to prevent infection.

• • • • • • • • • •

Would you rather
create a natural mosquito repellent from essential oils or make a natural suncreen using natural oils?

Winner:

Did you know? Some plants, like aloe vera and coconut oil, contain natural SPF properties and have been used for centuries to protect skin from the sun.

Would you rather

Would you rather carve a spoon from wood or fashion a knife from a broken piece of glass?

Winner:

Did you know? Glass knives, also known as "flintknapped" knives, were used by early humans for cutting and butchering before the discovery of metal.

• • • • • • • • • •

Would you rather

learn to make a bow and arrow from branches or construct a shelter using a tarp and paracord?

Winner:

Did you know? Paracord, originally used in parachutes during World War II, is now popular among outdoor enthusiasts for its strength and versatility.

Would you rather
learn to make a rope ladder from vines or fashion a digging tool from a sharpened stick?

Winner:

Did you know? Rope ladders made from vines have been used by ancient civilizations for accessing cliff dwellings, treehouses, and caves.

• • • • • • • • • •

Would you rather
create an SOS signal using brightly colored clothing or a signal panel from a reflective emergency blanket?

Winner:

Did you know? Emergency blankets, made from reflective material, are often used to retain body heat in survival situations but can also be used to create visible signals for rescue.

Would you rather
rather forage for wild berries or hunt for edible mushrooms in the forest?

Winner:

Did you know? Many wild berries, such as blueberries and raspberries, are rich in antioxidants and vitamins, making them nutritious snacks in the wild.

• • • • • • • • • •

Would you rather
collect edible insects like crickets or search for wild edible roots like cattails?

Winner:

Did you know? Insects are a highly sustainable and protein-rich food source, with over 2,000 species known to be edible by humans.

METEROLOGICAL marvels

Would you rather
camp under the brightest full moon or during the most colorful sunset?

Winner:

Did you know? The brightest full moon is called a "supermoon" because it appears larger and brighter than usual!

• • • • • • • • • •

Would you rather
face a sudden snowstorm or a quick summer downpour while hiking?

Winner:

Did you know? Snowstorms can drop more than 2 feet of snow, while summer downpours are the heaviest rainfalls!

Would you rather
hear constant thunder or see non-stop lightning while in a tent?

Winner:

Did you know? Lightning can heat the air around it to temperatures five times hotter than the sun's surface!

• • • • • • • • • •

Would you rather
experience the strongest wind you've ever felt or the heaviest rain during a campout?

Winner:

Did you know? Winds can travel faster than a cheetah can run, reaching speeds over 60 miles per hour!

Would you rather
have a snowball fight in a blizzard or dance in the rain during a thunderstorm?

Winner:

Did you know? Thunderstorms can produce over 3,000 lightning strikes in a single day!

● ● ● ● ● ● ● ● ● ●

Would you rather
watch a volcano erupting from a safe distance or a tornado forming while you're camping?

Winner:

Did you know? Tornadoes can spin as fast as 300 miles per hour, making them nature's most powerful twisters!

Would you rather
wear a raincoat all day in misty weather or sunglasses in a desert-like heatwave?

Winner:

Did you know? The highest temperature ever recorded was 134°F in Death Valley, California!

● ● ● ● ● ● ● ● ● ●

Would you rather
build a snowman in sub-zero temperatures or a sandcastle in scorching heat?

Winner:

Did you know? Snow can act as an insulator, keeping things warmer than the outside air in extreme cold!

Would you rather
canoe in a gentle rain or
windsurf during a breezy day?

Winner:

Did you know? Windsurfing sails can catch winds going more than 25 miles per hour, turning a breezy day into a speedy adventure!

● ● ● ● ● ● ● ● ● ●

Would you rather
hike through a dense fog or a heavy hailstorm?

Winner:

Did you know? Hailstones can grow as large as a grapefruit during severe storms!

Would you rather
fly a kite in strong winds or build a fort during a heavy snowfall?

Winner:

Did you know? The record for the highest altitude a kite has flown is over 16,000 feet, which is higher than some mountains!

• • • • • • • • • •

Would you rather
have an ice cream in scorching heat or hot chocolate in freezing cold?

Winner:

Did you know? Hot chocolate was first made by the Mayans over 2000 years ago!

Would you rather
find shelter from a sudden tornado or from a rapidly rising flood?

Winner:

Did you know? Floodwaters can rise so quickly, they are capable of lifting cars off the ground!

• • • • • • • • • •

Would you rather
walk through a calm snowfall or a gentle rain?

Winner:

Did you know? No two snowflakes are exactly the same, each one is uniquely shaped!

Would you rather
watch clouds forming shapes or the wind swaying giant trees?

Winner:

Did you know? Clouds can weigh more than a million pounds, and you can see them floating because they are spread over such a large area!

• • • • • • • • • •

Would you rather
jump in puddles during a spring shower or crunch leaves in a crisp fall breeze?

Winner:

Did you know? Leaves change color in fall due to reduced sunlight, which causes the green chlorophyll to disappear!

Would you rather
be out in the sun during the hottest day of the year or the coldest night?

Winner:

Did you know? The coldest temperature ever recorded on Earth was minus 128 degrees Fahrenheit in Antarctica!

• • • • • • • • • •

Would you rather
explore a misty mountain or a sunny beach?

Winner:

Did you know? Mountains can create their own weather systems, which is why they're often misty!

Would you rather
witness the formation of a rainbow or the dance of the northern lights?

Winner:

Did you know? Rainbows happen because light bends and spreads out into colors like a fan when it passes through raindrops, creating a beautiful arc in the sky!

• • • • • • • • • •

Would you rather
wear a heavy coat in a light snow or a t-shirt in a cool breeze?

Winner:

Did you know? Light snow can accumulate quickly, sometimes creating a winter wonderland in just hours!

Would you rather
camp in a desert with a rare rain shower or in a rainforest during a dry spell?

Winner:

Did you know? Deserts can go years without rain, but when it rains, it can transform the landscape overnight!

• • • • • • • • • •

Would you rather
chase a waterfall in a rainy season or a comet in a clear night sky?

Winner:

Did you know? Comets are cosmic snowballs of frozen gases, rock, and dust that orbit the Sun!

Would you rather
listen to the symphony of cracking glacier ice or roaring monsoon rains?

Winner:

Did you know? Glaciers are massive and can make sounds that echo through valleys when they crack!

• • • • • • • • • •

Would you rather
plant a tree in a windy area or a rainy one?

Winner:

Did you know? Trees planted in windy areas often grow stronger as they resist the forces of the wind!

Would you rather
see a dust devil on a hike or a water spout while boating?

Winner:

Did you know? Water spouts are like tornadoes over water, and dust devils are mini whirlwinds on land!

● ● ● ● ● ● ● ● ● ●

Would you rather
try to outrun a slow-moving fog or a fast-moving cloud shadow?

Winner:

Did you know? Fog moves slowly and can engulf entire landscapes, while cloud shadows can travel quickly across the ground with the moving sun!

Would you rather
wear snowshoes in a deep winter snow or rain boots in a muddy spring rain?

Winner:

Did you know? Snowshoes distribute your weight over a larger area to prevent sinking into the snow, much like how rain boots prevent your feet from getting wet and muddy!

● ● ● ● ● ● ● ● ● ●

Would you rather
spend a day in the humid jungle or a dry desert?

Winner:

Did you know? Jungles can have humidity levels up to 90%, making them some of the wettest places on earth!

Would you rather
see a comet passing close to Earth or a total solar eclipse?

Winner:

Did you know? Total solar eclipses completely block the Sun's light, turning day into night for a brief and magical moment!

• • • • • • • • • •

Would you rather
camp in a place where you can see the aurora every night or where you can watch shooting stars every night?

Winner:

Did you know? Auroras are nature's light shows, created when solar wind clashes with Earth's magnetic field, lighting up the sky in dazzling colors.

Would you rather
swim in a bioluminescent bay at night or watch an aurora from a snowy mountain?

Winner:

Did you know? Bioluminescence is caused by microorganisms in the water that emit light, creating a magical glow similar to the natural light display of auroras!

• • • • • • • • • •

Would you rather
camp in a place where you can see the aurora every night or where you can watch shooting stars every night?

Winner:

Did you know? Both auroras and shooting stars are best viewed from dark, remote areas away from city lights!

This Certificate Is Presented To

. . . ______________________________ . . .

Made in United States
North Haven, CT
24 June 2024